The Truth about
Great White
SHARKS

Written by Mary M. Cerullo   Photographs by Jeffrey L. Rotman   Illustrations by Michael Wertz

chronicle books · san francisco

Gleaming white teeth

and coal black eyes:

This is what people who have come face-to-face with a **great white shark** remember most.

hello, my name is SHARK

Scientists and photographers who have met a great white shark admire this awesome animal. But people who only know this shark by reputation fear it. No other animal stirs up emotions like the great white shark. And no other animal has had so much written about it based on so few facts.

Great white sharks are a mystery even to shark scientists because they are so hard to study. They can't be kept in a fish tank for observation. So far, no great white shark has lived more than a few days in an aquarium. Researchers sometimes have to hunt for weeks to find them in the ocean. When the sharks do appear, often lured by the scent of blood, researchers must observe them from inside the safety of a shark cage. Usually, the sharks eat the food hung out to attract them and then disappear into the shadows. Researchers can only guess at what great whites do away from their view—how far they travel, where they give birth, or how many live in the ocean.

A shark cage is like an underwater elevator enclosed by strong bars on all sides. Floats on the top help the cage stay at the surface in case it gets torn from the steel cables that attach it to the boat's deck.

Once when underwater photographers Ron and Valerie Taylor were in a shark cage, a 12-foot (4-meter) great white became tangled in the cable and dragged the cage underwater. The floats kept it from sinking, but they had a wild ride until the shark became tired from struggling to escape. Ron and the boat crew cut it free and the shark swam off.

By counting the growth rings
(like tree rings) in cross-
sections of shark backbones,
scientists have learned that
great whites may live 25 to
30 years or longer. Other
researchers are tracing
the great white's family
tree using DNA testing
of shark skin samples.
They hope to learn
whether great whites
in one area of the
ocean are closely related
to those in another area.
Although there is much
more to learn, what scientists have already discovered
about great white sharks may
change the way people feel
about these "monsters" of
the sea.

Like detectives, ocean biologists are slowly piecing together clues that reveal the true nature of great white sharks. These researchers are learning about how great white sharks survive in the sea, how they behave when they're hunting or having babies, and what humans need to do to protect them.

Marine biologists attach tags to great white sharks to find out where they go. Each tag has a different number on it, and the researchers record the number and where and when the shark was tagged before releasing the shark. If someone catches the shark again later, the numbered tag lets the scientists know how far the shark has traveled. Some tags have ultrasonic transmitters that allow researchers to track the shark's movements.

The Great White Shark Is Not the Biggest Living Shark

Basking shark

Two other kinds of sharks are bigger than the great white. Basking sharks grow to be 40 feet (12 meters) long and whale sharks grow up to 50 feet (15 meters) long; that makes them as long as a school bus. You would think these huge animals eat almost anything, but they actually feed on some of the smallest animals in the sea. Both the basking shark and the whale shark eat small shrimplike creatures called krill, which are no longer than your finger.

Whale shark

MARK METERS FEET

5 6 7 8 9 10 11 12 13 14

Shark

How Do You Measure a Great White Shark?

From time to time, fishermen in Australia, California, and the Mediterranean have reported catching great white sharks 23 feet (7 meters) long or longer, but scientists doubt these stories. They think maybe the fishermen didn't measure the sharks the way scientists do. But even scientists don't agree on the right way to measure a great white shark. Do you measure from its snout to the tip of its tail? Do you measure to the fork in the middle of the tail? Some measurements don't even include the tail! So how do you know how long a shark really is?

Most will tell you to do it this way:

When a shark is laid out on the deck of a boat, measure a straight line from the tip of its snout to the end of the upper lobe of its tail. Don't place your tape measure across the body of the shark. That will make the shark seem longer. Measure along the deck.

While great whites are not as long as their cousins, the basking shark and whale shark, they are solid and bulky, built like football players. Jeff Rotman, who took the photographs in this book, has swum with many different kinds of sharks. He was impressed not just by the length but by the width of great white sharks. "Great whites are huge," he says. "They move through the water like trucks!"

Some great whites grow to 19 to 21 feet (about 6 meters) long and weigh as much as 7,000 pounds (3,175 kilograms) or about twice as much as a pick-up truck! Most, however, are about 12 to 16 feet (4 to 5 meters) long or about the size of a family minivan.

To get a sense of how big a great white is, take a tape measure and s t r e t c h   i t   o u t   1 6   f e e t. Then unroll it to 21 feet.

BIG!

ONE

TWO

THREE

FOUR

5

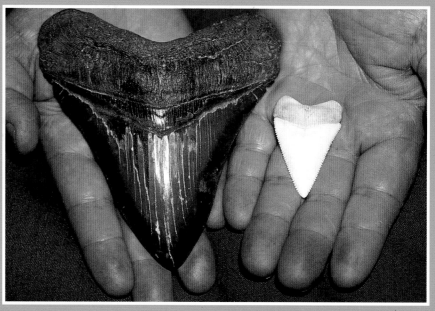

A megalodon's tooth next to a great white's tooth.

Megalodon

If you doubled the size of a great white, it would look like its ancestor, the megalodon, which lived from 50 to 4½ million years ago. *Carcharodon megalodon* was at least twice as long as the largest great white. While some shark lovers secretly hope megalodons still roam the unexplored depths of the ocean, most people are content to believe that the megalodon is extinct.

The only evidence we have that a megalodon once swam the seas is its teeth. From teeth the size of a man's hand, scientists have been able to build a model of what its jaws and the rest of its body probably looked like. Scientists have concluded that the megalodon was about 45 to 50 feet (15 meters) long and weighed more than 20 tons. (That's as much as five elephants.)

Modern and Ancient Great Whites

Many shark teeth are found on the ocean floor. White teeth are from sharks that live today; brown or black ones are fossilized teeth from sharks that lived long ago. Like dinosaurs' bones, these teeth became fossilized when they were buried in the mud at the bottom of an ancient sea. Minerals from the ocean water seeped into the teeth and turned them to stone.

Why do we find

only the teeth of the extinct megalodon? All other parts of a shark's skeleton are made of soft material called cartilage that rots away before it can become fossilized.

What's in a Name?

Maybe because the great white shark is pointed on both ends, it is known in South Africa as "blue pointer" or "uptail." South Africans also call it "tommy." In Australia it is known as "white pointer" or the more frightful, "white death." Often they are simply called "white sharks."

Scientists around the world call them *Carcharodon carcharias*, which is Greek for "ragged tooth shark." This way scientists can always agree on what animal they're talking about no matter what great whites are called locally.

Great White Sharks Are Fish

If you stopped people on the street and asked them, most would say sharks aren't fish. But sharks are indeed fish. Most fish, such as tuna, swordfish, and guppies, have skeletons made of hard bone. Ichthyologists, scientists who study fish, call them "bony fish." Instead of bone, sharks' skeletons are made of a softer material called cartilage. This is why ichthyologists put sharks, rays, skates, and chimaeras in their own special group called cartilaginous fish. We have cartilage in our ears, ankles, and the tips of our noses.

Few fish are as well-designed as sharks. It's not surprising since they've had over 450 million years to get it right. Sharks and their ancestors existed before the bony fish. Sharks ruled the ancient seas when dinosaurs roamed the land.

Here are **three** of the qualities that make the great white shark a top predator of the sea.

1 Conveyor Belt of Teeth

Watching a great white shark eat is an unforgettable sight. When a shark bites, it thrusts out its lower jaw to open its mouth extra wide. This action reveals 26 upper teeth and 24 lower teeth, with row after row of smaller teeth lined up behind them. Because they are set loosely into a jaw of cartilage, the teeth can fall out but they are quickly replaced. At any time, about a third of the teeth are growing back. A single great white shark may lose thousands of teeth in its lifetime. (Imagine how busy a shark tooth fairy would be!)

The teeth of great white sharks are shaped like triangles. They have jagged edges like a saw blade to saw through tough meat, and they do this very well. In about a second, a great white can cut a 20-pound slice out of its prey. While adult great whites have cutting teeth, young great whites have narrower, pointier teeth, for spearing smaller fish and other kinds of sharks.

2 | Armored Skin

A great white shark's skin is rough like sandpaper. If you stroked a great white shark toward its tail, the skin would feel smooth. If you rubbed forward toward the shark's head, you would scrape your hand. A microscope reveals that the great white's skin is covered by rows and rows of tiny, pointed daggers called denticles. Denticles means "skin teeth" because they are made of the same material as shark teeth. Not much can pierce the tough skin of a shark, not even the teeth of its victims or the bite of another shark during mating.

3 | Super Senses

Sharks have the same senses that humans have: hearing, sight, touch, taste, and smell. Some kinds of sharks hear their prey first. Others use their nose to pick up the scent given off by a bleeding or frightened fish. Then they may catch sight of their prey. Great white sharks seem to use a combination of these senses, depending on the kind (fish or seal) and condition (alive or dead) of the next meal. They can see color, and marine biologists think that great whites may see objects at a distance better than ones that are close up.

The shark's sense of touch also comes into play. Like other fish, a great white shark has a lateral line, or a row of tiny holes that runs from head to tail. This "distant touch" picks up vibrations in the water. The lateral line can feel an approaching school of fish or sense another shark moving in on its prey.

A great white shark can find a fish even if it is buried in the sand. It senses the faint electricity given off by a pumping heart or beating gills. Every living thing gives off a weak electric field that the shark can sense through tiny holes in its snout and chin. If you look closely at a shark you will see the holes, named the ampullae of Lorenzini after one of the shark scientists who discovered the tiny, jelly-filled pores in the 1600s.

Great white sharks are extremely sensitive to electric currents, which makes it difficult to keep them in captivity. They sense the electricity given off by the pumps, lights, and metal of an aquarium tank. All these signals confuse them, causing the sharks to run into walls and hurt themselves.

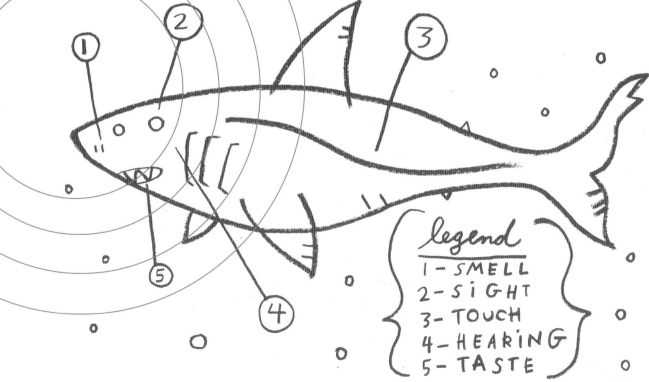

legend

1 - SMELL
2 - SIGHT
3 - TOUCH
4 - HEARING
5 - TASTE

Great Whites Are Not Cold-Blooded Killers

How are sharks different from bony fish?

Bony Fish		Sharks
gill flap	•	5–7 rows of gills
one or two sets of teeth	•	many rows of teeth replace a tooth soon after it falls out
scales	•	denticles ("skin teeth")
swimbladder	•	no swimbladder—sinks when stops swimming
skeleton of bone	•	skeleton of cartilage

In fact, great whites can be surprisingly warm. Mammals, including humans, are warm-blooded, which means they keep their bodies at a constant temperature. The body temperature of a healthy human stays around 98.6° F (37° C) whether she is in the tropics or in the Arctic. By contrast, most fish are cold-blooded creatures, which means that they take on the temperature of the water in which they are swimming. But great white sharks are fish that can raise their body temperature like warm-blooded animals.

John McCosker and other shark scientists discovered this fact by feeding great whites meat in which they had hidden thermometers hooked to radio transmitters. They learned that a great white shark can raise its stomach temperature as much as 7°F and its muscle temperature as much as 5°F higher than the surrounding water. This increases the shark's speed and reaction time, like a runner who has already warmed up before a race. It also helps the shark digest its food faster. It's all the more impressive when you consider that great white sharks are usually found in the cooler regions of the world's oceans.

Flat Sharks

Rays and skates are close relatives of sharks. You can think of them as flattened sharks whose side fins have expanded into "wings" that glide over the ocean floor. Except for the manta ray, which swims near the surface scooping small fish and plankton into its gaping mouth, they stay close to the ocean floor. Their shape and coloring help them blend in with the sand. Some sharks, such as the angel shark, are also shaped to hug the ocean bottom.

Great Whites Are Good Mothers

Many bony fish lay millions of eggs and then abandon them. But great white sharks have only a few babies at a time, which they keep inside their bodies for many months. The baby sharks hatch from eggs while they are still inside their mother. When they are born, they are fully formed and ready to fend for themselves.

Scientists think great white sharks don't begin having babies until they are at least 10 to 12 years old. Like other sharks, great whites may have only one litter every two years, and each litter contains only a few pups.

Although mother great whites have "litters" and the newborns are called "pups," baby great whites would never be called "cute." Marine biologists suspect that some great white sharks start hunting even before they leave their mother! They have found many more egg cases inside a female great white than the 5 to 10 pups that eventually are born. Like the pups of a few other large shark species, the first-born great white pup may feast on its brothers and sisters as they pop out of their egg cases.

The great white shark babies that live long enough to be born are ready to hunt and care for themselves. At birth, a great white shark is about 4 feet (1.2 meters) long and weighs about 40 pounds (18 kilograms) or the size of a human kindergartner.

Great Whites Don't Attack in a Feeding Frenzy

In order to attract great white sharks to their research boats, scientists pour blood, fish oil, meat, and tuna into the water. Bringing together lots of great whites in one place and filling the water with blood would seem to be the perfect set-up for a feeding frenzy. Other kinds of sharks sometimes attack each other when competing for food. But that doesn't happen with great white sharks. They just calmly gobble up the chunks of tuna offered by the researchers. Smaller sharks, though, are wise to stay away from great white shark feeding areas. Otherwise they may find themselves becoming part of the meal!

Great White Sharks Can Jump

Great whites do some strange things while they are hunting. They have been seen poking their heads out of the water, perhaps to look around for seals sunning themselves on rocks.

Recently scientists have seen what fishermen having been telling them for years: great whites sharks can leap nearly out of the water to pursue their prey. Off the coasts of California and South Africa, researchers have photographed great whites jumping straight out of the water. Usually the sharks were attacking their natural prey—seals or sea lions that may leap out of the water themselves to escape their enemies. Other times the sharks were chasing plastic decoys that researchers towed behind their boats.

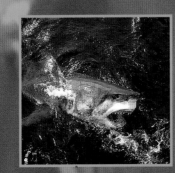

Great White Sharks Aren't Lurking Just Beyond the Waves (U s u a l l y)

"Jaws," the famous movie about a great white shark that terrorizes a coastal town, scared audiences so much that many people stopped swimming in the ocean after seeing it. In some seaside resorts, police had to patrol beaches where there had never been a shark attack to look out for sharks, just so beachgoers would feel safe.

Great white sharks will sometimes follow their prey up to the shoreline, but usually only around the few beaches that are well-known for shark attacks. Great whites visit the coasts of northern California, South Africa, and southern Australia when seals, sea lions, and elephant seals come onto land to give birth.

Great whites roam the cool waters of the world's oceans but they aren't common anywhere. Although great whites will come together to feed on the same prey, they usually don't travel in schools or even in pairs.

Great white sharks are loners.

The Truth Is...

Great White Sharks Aren't "Man-Eaters"

Each year there are about 50 shark attacks around the world, and in about 10 cases, the victims die. Up to half of these attacks have been blamed on great white sharks. Although the great white is the most feared shark, other sharks are called "man-eaters," too, including the tiger shark, hammerhead, bull shark, and oceanic whitetip shark.

Great whites occasionally do eat humans, but more often, they take one bite and leave. Because of this, great whites should probably not be called "man-eaters." "Man-biters" would be a better term.

Great whites attack people more often when they are near the surface of the ocean than on the bottom, so surfers, swimmers, kayakers, and divers returning to their dive boat are in the greatest danger. Unlike other sharks that hunt at dawn or dusk, great white sharks hunt during the day. That is also when their prey (seals and sea lions) are more likely to be in the water. Unfortunately, that is also when most humans are in the water.

Great White Sharks Attack with a Plan

Reports of great white shark attacks on people are surprisingly alike. In most cases, the shark appears without warning, takes a bite out of its victim, and then disappears. Some scientists think that sharks attack humans by mistake, since surfers on their boogie boards and divers in their wetsuits and flippers look a lot like the great white's favorite meals—sea lions and seals. Shark experts are also trying to figure out why so many people survive an attack. Why didn't the shark just gobble up the person when it had the chance? Did the shark realize its mistake? Maybe it didn't like the taste of human flesh.

Scientist John McCosker, an expert on great white sharks, has another theory. He has watched how a great white attacks an elephant seal that may weigh several thousand pounds. He says, "It mugs it. The shark sneaks up from below, attacks the body, and backs off to a safe distance until the animal bleeds to death." This way the shark isn't hurt by the tusks and claws of the struggling animal.

John calls this his "bite and spit" theory. The shark releases its victim and waits for it to stop moving. After a few minutes, the shark returns to eat its meal. But in most attacks on humans, the victim is rescued before the shark can return.

John McCosker and great white in the roundabout.

Al Giddings Images, Inc.

The Man Who Loves Sharks

John McCosker was the director of the Steinhart Aquarium in San Francisco. He lives along a part of the California coast known as the "shark attack capital of the world," making it one of the best places to study great whites. John met his first great white when he was fishing for rock cod off the Farallon Islands about 25 miles (40 kilometers) west of San Francisco. The shark rubbed up against John's boat, lifting it slightly out of the water. Then the great white swam up next to the 17-foot-long boat, turned on its side, and looked up at John. At that moment, John was sure the shark was twice as big as his boat. After returning to shore, though, he decided it was only half that size.

John's goal was to make Steinhart Aquarium the first place to keep a great white shark in captivity. To do that he designed and built a "roundabout." It's a donut-shaped tank without any corners in it so that the shark can swim without bumping into walls.

Sharks Prefer Fatty Foods

Shark researcher A. Peter Klimley has a different explanation for why more people aren't killed by great white sharks. He thinks great whites don't usually eat humans because we aren't fat enough for them. Great whites eat fish, squid, dolphins, seals, elephant seals, sea lions, and even dead whales. Sometimes they spit out things they might be expected to eat, such as pelicans, penguins, sea otters, and humans. He says, "Most great white attacks on humans or pelicans seem to end with the shark spitting out the creature it mistook for its normal prey—although sometimes too late to keep the victim from bleeding to death.... They strongly prefer seals, sea lions, and whale carcasses…which they seek for their high fat content." Eating these plump prey can help keep a great white going for weeks or even a month without eating again, as it lives off the stored fat in its liver.

Like all predators, great whites go after the animals that are easiest to catch: the old, the sick, the weak, and the young. Because great white sharks rid the ocean of sick and dying animals, shark supporter Rodney Fox calls them the "great feeding and cleaning machines of the deep."

How Much Wood Would a Great White Chuck?

Great whites sometimes bite boats and logs. Sharks have no hands, so they have to use their jaws to examine an object they don't recognize. If it turns out to be something good to eat, they keep on munching. If not, they will spit it out. Great whites sometimes bite at the bars of a shark cage. Rather than trying to reach the humans inside, they may just be trying to find out what the cage tastes like!

yummy!

Great White Sharks Aren't White

One of the things that spooks people who are diving with great whites is that the animals seem to appear suddenly out of nowhere. One minute the ocean is empty in every direction, and the next thing you know, a great white shark is nibbling at the bars of your shark cage.

Camouflage may be key to the shark's ability to sneak up on divers. A great white shark is only white on its underbelly. It is dark gray on top. Viewed from underneath, the white belly blends in with the sunlit surface water. From above, the gray back disappears against the dark shadows of the ocean depths. This two-toned color pattern is called countershading. Dolphins, sea gulls, penguins, and many fish have the same coloring. Countershading is useful for hiding from predators. Great whites don't have any predators, but counter-shading helps disguise them from their prey.

Far-Out Facts

You have a better chance of dying from a bee sting than from a shark attack. You also are far more likely to be killed by a tornado, a lightning bolt, or even falling airplane parts. In fact, in the United States fewer than a dozen people go to the hospital each year because of shark bites, while over 500 go with injuries from handling Christmas ornaments.

Does this mean that bees and Christmas ornaments are more dangerous than sharks? Think about the facts behind these statistics. Isn't it more likely you will meet a bee than a shark? How many people put up Christmas trees each year compared to how many people swim or surf in the ocean? How badly were the victims hurt?

Sometimes people connect facts to make conclusions that don't really make sense when you look at them closely. The fact is, sharks can be dangerous, and when you intrude in their world, you should treat them with respect!

DANGER

The Great White Shark Has Only One Enemy...and it Is Us

The great white is an apex predator, which means it is at the top of the food chain. Nothing else eats it. Other apex predators of the sea include killer whales and sperm whales. Apex predators on land include lions, tigers, bears, and humans. Even though nothing in the ocean threatens great white sharks, they are in danger—from humans. Fishermen snag them in their nets. Big-game hunters hook them, harpoon them, and shoot them to win trophies. Others kill them to sell their jaws for as much as U.S. $5,000 apiece.

The death of each great white shark is important because great whites aren't easy to replace. They grow slowly and have few babies. We don't know how many great white sharks can be taken from the ocean without endangering the whole population.

Conservation laws that forbid the killing of great whites may be the only way to keep them from becoming extinct. South Africa, Australia, and California now have laws that protect great white sharks. But great whites don't just stay in the few places they are protected, so some people believe the United Nations should take action to protect them worldwide.

Great White Sharks Do Have Friends

Great whites need more friends like Rodney Fox, a conservationist who has been keeping track of the number of great whites around southern Australia for many years. He knows many individuals by sight, identifying them by their peculiar scars or notches on their fins. He also tags them so they can be identified when they are caught again later on or in another location. He guesses there are no more than 250 great whites left along Australia's southern coast.

What would happen to the ocean if it lost its top predator? Who would do their job of removing sick and weak animals from the ocean? It is possible we would see marine mammals like seals and sea lions increase in number until they died of starvation or sickness.

We also have to wonder how the loss of these animals would affect humans. We are just beginning to discover some of the value sharks have for us.

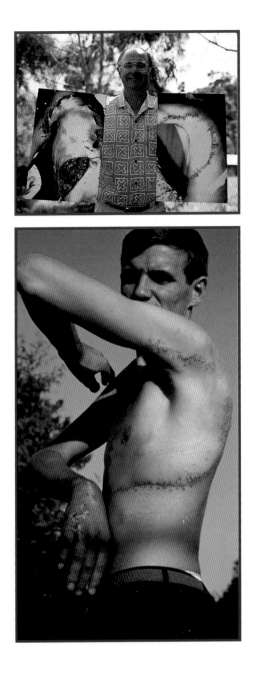

Rodney Fox cares a lot about the great white sharks of Australia, although his friendship with great whites did not get off to a good start. When Rodney was 23 years old, he was in a spear-fishing contest. He had a string of fish attached to his belt and was just taking aim at the largest prize yet, when he felt a force like a freight train hit his side. His spear gun was knocked from his hands. Although he couldn't see his attacker, he knew he was in the jaws of a great white shark. Rodney punched the place where the shark's eyes should be. The shark let go for a second. Rodney couldn't think of anything else to do so he wrapped his arms around the giant shark's jaws to try to keep it from biting him again. After a few seconds, he had to let go to kick for the surface to breathe.

Then came the scariest moment—He looked down and saw the shark rushing up from below, its jaws wide open. Rodney kicked at the shark's snout with all his might. The shark dove, taking Rodney's catch of speared fish with it. Rodney's friends came to the rescue and took him to the hospital. There, doctors put 462 stitches in his chest, arm, and hand.

After his attack, Rodney hated great whites. But he gradually began to realize that the shark wasn't a blood-thirsty killer, just an animal looking for a meal. Now Rodney takes scientists and photographers to meet the great white sharks so they can help others understand them better. As Rodney learned himself after surviving his first encounter with a great white shark, "To conquer fear is the beginning of wisdom."

The Truth Is...
Humans Need Sharks

Sharks have been helping humans for hundreds of years. People used to swallow a spoonful of bad-tasting shark-liver oil every day to keep them healthy. Until 1947, shark-liver oil was the main source for vitamin A. (Luckily, today we have vitamins.) Sharks have been used to make soaps, soup, lipsticks, sandpaper, and boots and purses.

Today, medical researchers are looking for other ways that sharks may help people. Shark cartilage, the flexible material that makes up their skeleton, has been used to help make an artificial skin to protect burn victims from infection while their own skin heals. Shark corneas have been transplanted into human eyes.

Manufacturers of pills and powders made from shark parts recommend them to treat human ailments from constipation to cancer, but doctors are more cautious. Chemicals found in the liver, stomach, and gallbladder of sharks have stopped the growth of human tumors in some laboratory experiments, which raises the hope that sharks may one day help to cure cancer. Other people are studying sharks to see how they might help treat heart and kidney diseases. Researchers hope someday to solve the mystery of how sharks are able to resist disease, but for now, it still puzzles the medical community.

Scientists have many more questions about great white sharks than they have answers. So far, they have been able to study only a small number of great white sharks—and most of those were dead. In years to come, shark researchers may learn more by following them in submarines or by watching them from underwater laboratories. Future scientists will make discoveries that will likely change what we believe today is true about great white sharks.

Sharks Don't Cure Cancer

Sharks almost never get cancer, even when scientists inject them with cancer-causing chemicals in the laboratory. So could sharks cure cancer in people? A lot of people have hoped so. Thousands of cancer patients in the United States have taken pills or powder made from shark cartilage to treat their tumors. Finally, a study was done to see if cartilage really helped. Sixty cancer patients were given shark cartilage powder for three months to see if it would help shrink their tumors. In not a single case did the patients' tumors go away or even get smaller. Still, medical researchers hope they may someday find a way to tap the sharks' resistance to disease to help treat cancer in humans.

Maybe one of those scientists will be you!

How Can You Help?

Find out about organizations that are working to protect sharks:

National Audubon Society
Living Oceans Program
550 South Bay Avenue
Islip, New York 11751
www.audubon.org

Center for Marine Conservation
1725 DeSales Street, NW
Suite 600
Washington, DC 20036
www.cmc-ocean.org

World Wildlife Fund
Endangered Seas Campaign
1250 24th St., NW
Washington, DC 20037
www.worldwildlife.org

Other Helpful Tips!

- **Keep the sharks' home clean.** By cutting down on garbage, fertilizers, gasoline, and cleaning products, you reduce the amount of harmful chemicals and wastes that can end up in our water and eventually make their way into the ocean.

- **Get involved.** Take part in a beach clean-up or a recycling program.

- **Find out if there are any laws protecting sharks where you live.** Many sharks are taken for food or for sport. In some cases, so many sharks are being caught that some species are getting close to extinction. Write to politicians and ask them what they are doing to help preserve sharks.

- **Share what you know.** You can change someone else's opinion of sharks by telling them why sharks are important to the ocean and to humans.

Glossary

ampullae of Lorenzini

sensory organs that detect weak electric currents. Named after one of their first discoverers, Stephan Lorenzini, who thought their shape looked like jars (ampullae) used by ancient Romans

apex predator

animal at the top of its food chain

bony fish

fish with hard skeletons

camouflage

any kind of coloring that helps an animal blend in with its surroundings

cartilage

a tough but flexible substance that forms the skeletons of sharks, skates, and rays

cartilaginous fish

a fish with a skeleton made of cartilage

cold-blooded

having a body temperature that changes with the surrounding air or water. Most fish, amphibians, and reptiles are cold-blooded

countershading

a kind of camouflage created by dark coloring above and light coloring below

denticle

small, toothlike covering on a shark's skin containing dentine, the same material as their teeth are made of

extinct

a species of plant or animal that has died out

food chain
a sequence (such as plant plankton, animal plankton, shrimp, fish) in which
each species feeds on the one below it

ichthyologist
a scientist who studies fishes

lateral line
a row of sensory organs along the length of a fish
that feels vibrations in the water, responsible for "distant touch"

marine mammals
a group of warm-blooded, air-breathing sea animals that includes
whales, dolphins, seals, sea lions, elephant seals, walruses, and sea otters

plankton
literally, "wanderer." The animals and plants that drift with the ocean currents
which include microscopic plants and animals as well as the larval stages of
many sea creatures, such as fish, crabs, and lobsters

predator
an animal that hunts and eats other animals

prey
an animal hunted and killed for food by a predator

swim bladder
a gas-filled sac in the body of most bony fish. A bony fish can adjust
the gases in the swimbladder to keep itself at a certain depth in the water
without having to swim

tumor
an abnormal growth of tissue

warm-blooded
having a body temperature that stays the same no matter what the temperature
of its surroundings

Bibliography

There are many fascinating books about sharks.

Here are a few titles, and you will find many more in your local library. Check the copyright date on the book to see when the book was published. In dynamic fields such as great white shark research, new discoveries are being made all the time that may change what we once believed to be true about these mysterious animals.

For young readers

I Didn't Know That Sharks Keep Losing Their Teeth, by Claire Llewellyn. Brookfield, CT: Copper Beech Books, 1998.

Sharks, by Ruth Berman. Minneapolis, MN: Carolrhoda Books, 1995.

Sharks: Challengers of the Deep, by Mary M. Cerullo. New York: Cobblehill, 1993.

For adults

Cousteau's Great White Shark, by Jean-Michel Cousteau and
Mose Richards. New York: Harry N. Abrams, 1993.

Discovering Sharks, by Samuel H. Gruber. Highlands, New
Jersey: American Littoral Society, 1990.

Great White Shark, by Richard Ellis and John E. McCosker.
New York: HarperCollins Publishers, 1991.

Great White Sharks: The Biology of Carcharodon carcharias,
by A. Peter Klimley and David G. Ainley. San Diego,
CA: Academic Press, 1996.

Index